I0796092

Muscogee

F.A. BIRD

Checkerboard Library

An Imprint of Abdo Publishing
abdobooks.com

ABDOBOOKS.COM
Published by Abdo Publishing, a division of ABDO, PO Box 398166, Minneapolis, Minnesota 55439.

Printed in the United States of America, North Mankato, Minnesota
102024
012025

Editor: Lauri Nelson
Design: Mighty Media, Inc.

Cover Photograph: Daniel Koglin/Shutterstock Images
Interior Photographs: Ad_hominem/Shutterstock Images, p. 7; Angel Wynn/NativeStock, pp. 11, 23, 25; Birmingham Museum of Art/Wikimedia Commons, p. 15; Courtesy of US National Park Service, p. 9; Heritage Art/Heritage Images/Getty Images, p. 17; Jeffrey Greenberg/Universal Images Group/Getty Images, p. 5; Lauren Petracca/AP Photo, p. 29; Lot 12920/Prints & Photographs Division/Library of Congress/LC-USZ62-111977, p. 27; renjelharvey photography/Shutterstock Images, p. 21; Sepia Times/Universal Images Group/Getty Images, p. 13; Visual Studies Workshop/Getty Images, p. 19

Library of Congress Control Number: 2024938799

Publisher's Cataloging-in-Publication Data
Names: Bird, F.A., author.
Title: Muscogee / by F.A. Bird
Description: Minneapolis, Minnesota : ABDO Publishing, 2025 | Series: Native American nations | Includes online resources and index.
Identifiers: ISBN 9781098296247 (lib. bdg.) | ISBN 9798384917359 (ebook)
Subjects: LCSH: Muscogee Indian--Juvenile literature. | Creek Indians--Juvenile literature. | Maskoki Indians--Juvenile literature. | Native Americans--Juvenile literature. | Indians of North America--Juvenile literature. | Indigenous peoples--Social life and customs--Juvenile literature. | Cultural anthropology--Juvenile literature.
Classification: DDC 973.0497--dc23

Contents

Homelands

The Muscogee traditionally lived in the southeastern region of the United States. Their homelands once spread across present-day Georgia and Alabama. Those who lived in present-day Georgia were called Lower Creeks. Those who lived in present-day Alabama were called Upper Creeks.

Muscogee homelands had many different features. Some areas contained mountains, forests, hills, valleys, rivers, lakes, and creeks. Other areas had marshes and swamps where birds, alligators, and poisonous snakes lived.

The Muscogee received the name Creek from European settlers. The settlers traded with Native Americans who lived near a part of the Ocmulgee River that the settlers called Ochese Creek. The traders soon began calling these Native Americans the Creek. But the people of this tribe call themselves Muscogee.

Ocmulgee Mounds National Historical Park in Macon, Georgia

Society

The Muscogee society was made up of several clans. They included Wind, Skunk, Beaver, Bear, Wolf, Bird, Fox, Panther, Wildcat, Potato, Alligator, Raccoon, Toad, and Deer clans. The clans linked people to each other and to the Natural World.

The Muscogee clans lived in large, permanent towns. At least one *micco* (MEEK-koh), or chief, led each town. He was a respected man whom the people selected. The chief made decisions for the town with the help of advisers.

Each town had a political and ceremonial center. In the center stood a large council house, a town square, and a large U-shaped field. Meetings, dances, games, and other ceremonial events took place there.

Muscogee towns were divided into red towns and white towns. The red towns were home to warriors. The white towns were home to peacemakers.

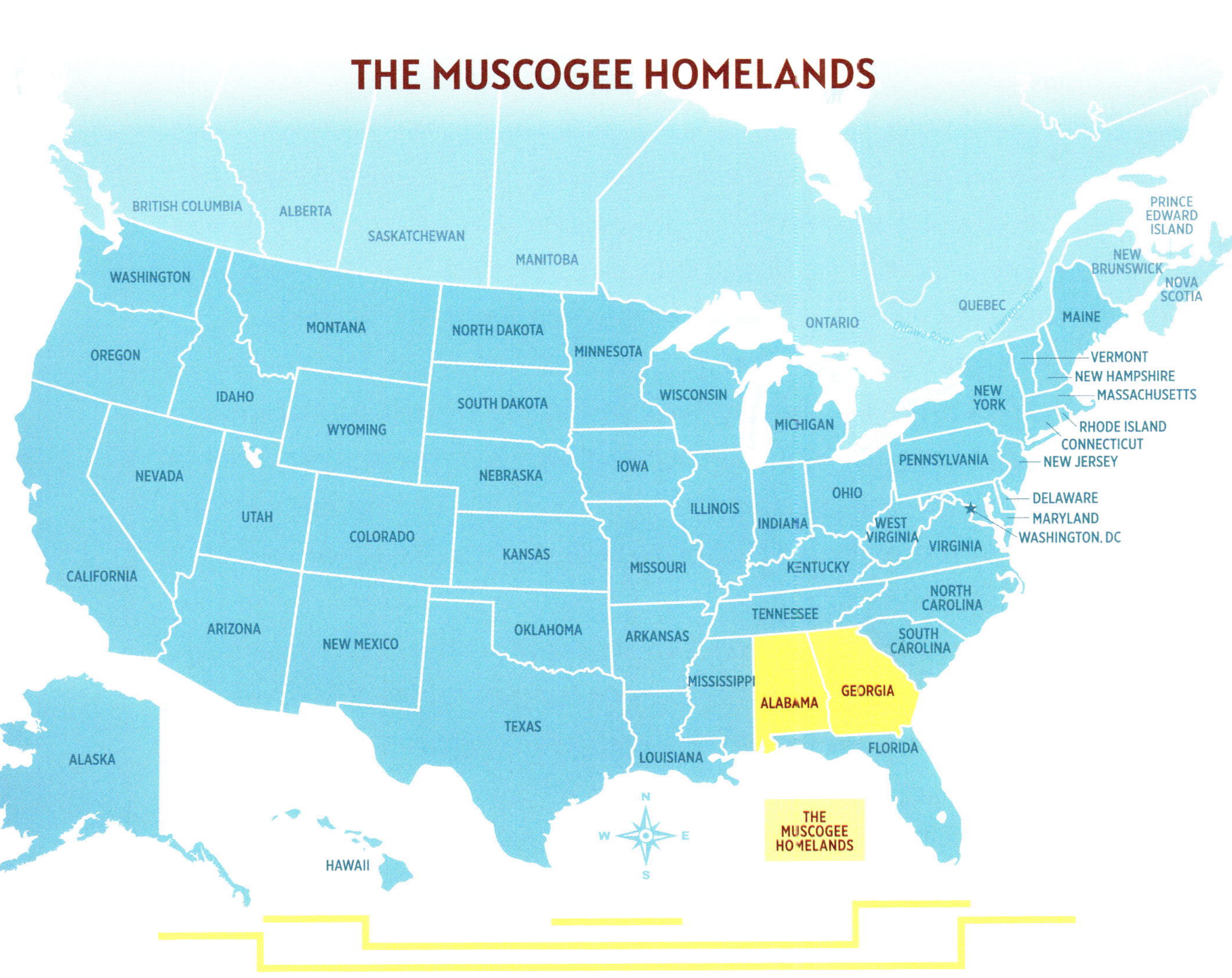
THE MUSCOGEE HOMELANDS
BRITISH COLUMBIA
ALBERTA
SASKATCHEWAN
MANITOBA
ONTARIO
QUEBEC
PRINCE EDWARD ISLAND
NEW BRUNSWICK
NOVA SCOTIA
Ottawa River
St. Lawrence River
WASHINGTON
OREGON
IDAHO
MONTANA
NORTH DAKOTA
MINNESOTA
WISCONSIN
MICHIGAN
NEW YORK
MAINE
VERMONT
NEW HAMPSHIRE
MASSACHUSETTS
RHODE ISLAND
CONNECTICUT
NEW JERSEY
PENNSYLVANIA
DELAWARE
MARYLAND
WASHINGTON, DC
SOUTH DAKOTA
WYOMING
NEBRASKA
IOWA
NEVADA
UTAH
COLORADO
ILLINOIS
INDIANA
OHIO
WEST VIRGINIA
VIRGINIA
CALIFORNIA
KANSAS
MISSOURI
KENTUCKY
NORTH CAROLINA
TENNESSEE
ARIZONA
NEW MEXICO
OKLAHOMA
ARKANSAS
SOUTH CAROLINA
MISSISSIPPI
ALABAMA
GEORGIA
TEXAS
LOUISIANA
FLORIDA
ALASKA
HAWAII
N
W
E
S
THE MUSCOGEE HOMELANDS

CHAPTER 3

Homes

Muscogee homes surrounded the ceremonial center of the town. Each family had a plot of land with room for several buildings. Some buildings stored food, others were winter homes, and still others were summer homes.

Winter and summer homes were rectangular. Winter homes had wooden frames and roofs woven out of vines and branches. The Muscogee plastered these structures with mud. The mud kept the heat inside during the winter. These homes had no windows. But there was a smoke hole in each roof.

Summer homes also had wooden frames. The frames held up thatched roofs. The Muscogee made the roofs by tying dried grass to the frames. These homes kept the people comfortable by letting in the cool night air.

The food storage buildings were usually two stories tall. They held baskets and containers filled with dried meat, fish, corn, and other foods. Tools were also stored here.

Houses in Muscogee towns were grouped around a plaza or community square. The plaza was a gathering place for ceremonies, doing business, and playing games.

Food

The Muscogee gathered, hunted, fished, and farmed. They gathered berries, nuts, herbs, and wild onions. The men hunted deer, bear, alligators, rabbits, squirrels, ducks, doves, and bobwhite quail. They hunted with bows and arrows, blowguns made from cane, and woven traps.

Muscogee homelands contained many rivers filled with fish. The Muscogee caught trout, bass, and catfish. Men fished with spears and lines tied to bone hooks. They also used woven twig fences to trap fish in shallow water.

The Muscogee grew corn, squash, beans, sweet potatoes, and pumpkins. They used hoes and planting sticks. The hoe was made from stone, or from a deer's shoulder bone attached to a long stick.

Deer meat and corn were the Muscogee's most important foods. The Muscogee stored the food they could not eat right away. They dried meat, fish, berries, and vegetables to eat in the winter.

Crops of beans, corn, and squash are also known as the Three Sisters.

CHAPTER 5

Clothing

The Muscogee made clothing from deerskins, plant fibers, and animal furs. Women used **awls**, bone needles, and **sinew** to make clothing.

Men wore deerskin **breechcloths** and leggings. They wore **sashes** that hung over one shoulder and tied at the waist. The sashes were woven from plant fibers.

Women wore deerskin dresses and skirts. They made these dresses by sewing two deer **hides** together. Women wore tops woven from plant fibers and rabbit fur.

Both men and women wore deerskin moccasins. They wore shawls woven from grass over their shoulders. To keep warm in the winter, the Muscogee wore fur robes.

Men **tattooed** their chests and faces. Sometimes they painted their faces, too. They made the face paint from minerals and plants. Men also wore turbans on their heads. Sometimes they placed feathers in their turbans. Muscogee men and women also wore earrings and necklaces.

Women made moccasins from a single piece of hide.

CHAPTER 6

Crafts

The Muscogee made beautiful, finger-woven sashes, belts, and cloth. To do this, they rolled plant fibers such as cotton, Indian hemp, and milkweed into strings. Sometimes they dyed the strings with plants and berries.

The women tied strings to a small, horizontal twig. They wove the strings back and forth to make a sash. Sometimes the women wove designs into the sashes. These included **geometric** shapes or nature designs.

The Muscogee made a special sash with a square pouch. The pouch had a triangular-shaped flap. They wore the sash over one shoulder. The sashes and pouches were **embroidered** with scroll designs. The scroll designs represented the Creator's breath.

After Europeans arrived in Muscogee homelands, the Muscogee began using trade goods to make and decorate their clothing. These goods included wool cloth and glass beads.

Muscogee bag decorated with spirals and designs from nature

CHAPTER 7

Family

Clans were important to Muscogee society. Clans brought people together as one big family. The Muscogee have a matrilineal society. This means that children belong to the clan of their mother.

The Muscogee had to "marry across the fire." This meant they could not marry someone from their own clan. People of the same clan, whether related by blood or not, were considered family.

When a man wanted to marry a woman, he gave her a gift. If she took the gift, it meant she agreed to marry him. The man moved into the woman's home. If the couple still wanted to marry after a year passed, a wedding was held.

Each person in the family had a role. Women tended to the children, farming, food, and clothing. Men hunted, fished, made tools, and protected the people. Elders kept the Muscogee history alive. They taught the children traditional ceremonies, songs, dances, and stories.

Tchoweeputokaw, a Muscogee woman

Children

Children learned skills from their mothers' sisters and brothers. Uncles taught the boys, and aunts taught the girls. This brought the extended family closer.

The uncles taught the boys many skills, such as how to hunt and fish. Boys learned how to make blowguns for hunting. They also watched the men make dugout canoes.

Girls helped care for younger children. They learned how to sew and finger weave. They helped their aunts prepare foods, such as corn dumplings and deer jerky.

Grandparents told stories to the children. Some stories made everyone laugh. Other stories were serious and taught the children lessons about Muscogee life.

Muscogee children also enjoyed playing games, such as chunkey. To play chunkey, one player rolled a round stone down the playing field. The other players threw long sticks to where they thought the stone would stop.

Two Seminole girls. Seminoles trace their origins from the Muscogee and other tribes from Florida, Georgia, and Alabama.

CHAPTER 9

Traditions

The Muscogee believe the Creator made them from red earth. They spread out in every direction. The Creator sent a blanket of fog over the earth that blinded the Muscogee. They stopped and called out to each other. By following the sounds of their voices, the Muscogee found each other.

Then the Creator took a deep breath and blew the fog away. He said to the Muscogee, "Now you see how important it is to stay together. The first thing you see will be your **clan**. All members of your clan will be family."

The Muscogee standing closest to the sun called themselves the Wind clan. They were the first to see the wind blow away the fog. Then each group saw things such as a panther, a snake, a potato, or an alligator. This is how each clan got its name.

The Muscogee call the Creator the Master-of-Breath, because he blew the fog away. He also taught the Muscogee an important lesson about family.

The Muscogee have 16 clans, including Wind, Bear, and Turtle.

War

The Muscogee went to war to avenge the killing of one of their people. They also fought to protect their lands. Muscogee warriors used blowguns, bows and arrows, knives, war clubs, and spears. The men often wore shell or bone **gorgets** on their necks. After they began to trade with Europeans, the Muscogee also used guns in battle.

In the early 1800s, a Shawnee chief named Tecumseh visited the Muscogee. He convinced some to join with northern tribes to fight against white settlers. These Muscogee warriors were called Red Sticks.

On August 30, 1813, the Red Sticks attacked Fort Mims. They killed several hundred men, women, and children. US General Andrew Jackson led troops on several attacks against the Muscogee. The most important was the Battle of Horseshoe Bend in 1814. The Muscogee lost this battle. They were forced to give 23 million acres of their homelands to the United States.

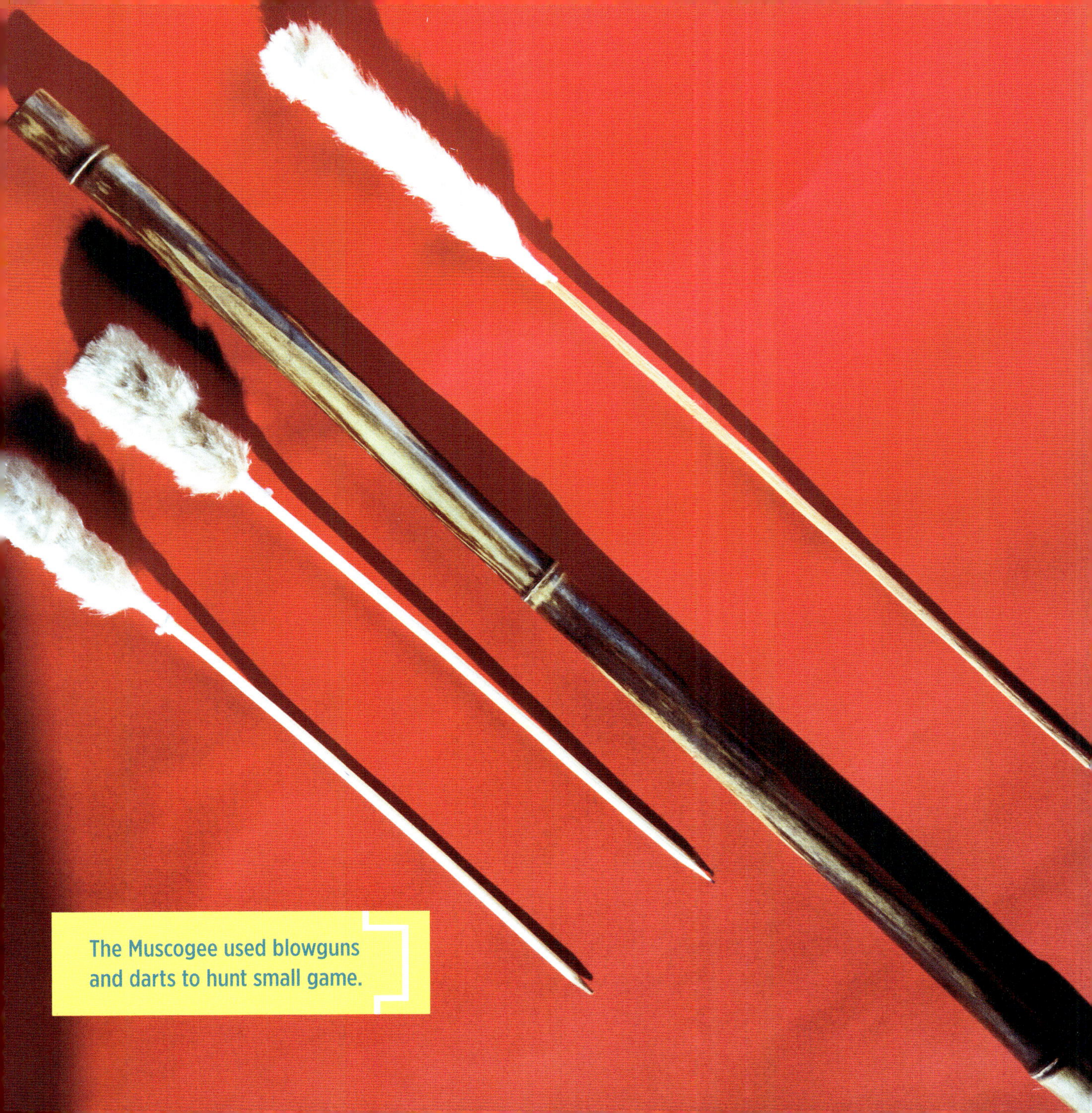

The Muscogee used blowguns and darts to hunt small game.

CHAPTER II

Contact with Europeans

The first contact between the Muscogee and Europeans was around 1540. Spanish explorer Hernando de Soto passed through Muscogee territory. The Muscogee traded for iron tools such as axes, hoes, and **adzes**.

In 1670, the English built Charles Town on Muscogee homelands. Charles Town became a trading center. The English wanted deerskins to be made into leather items. The Muscogee got cloth, glass beads, tin pots and pans, tools, guns, and ammunition.

In 1830, the Indian Removal Act became law. All Native Americans living east of the Mississippi River were to move to Indian Territory. In 1836, the US government forced Muscogee who had stayed on traditional homeland **allotments** to march to Indian Territory. Many died on the journey. Others traveled south to live with the Seminole.

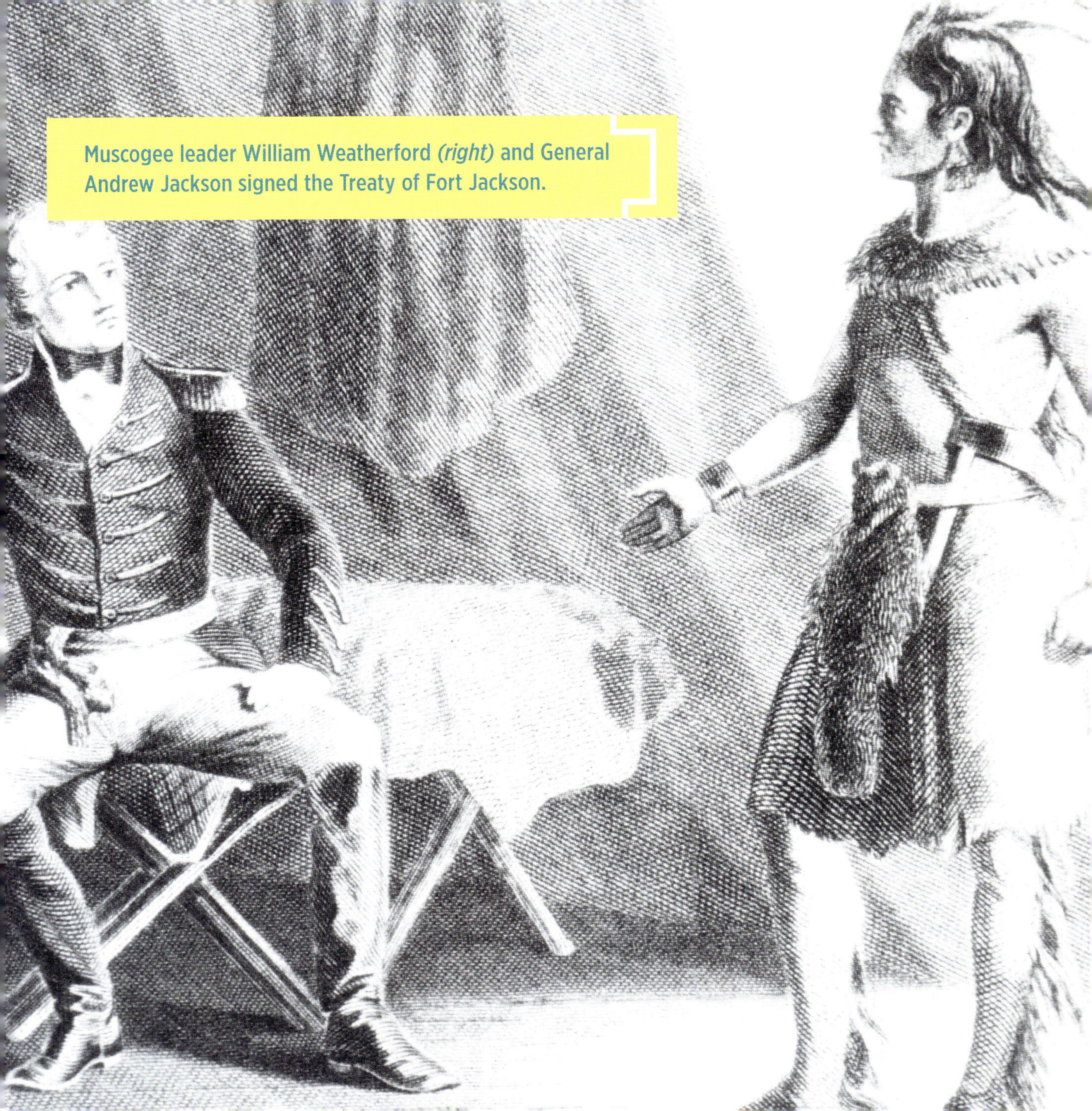

Muscogee leader William Weatherford *(right)* and General Andrew Jackson signed the Treaty of Fort Jackson.

Chitto Harjo

Chitto Harjo (chit-toe ha-cho) was a Muscogee chief. His name means Recklessly Brave Snake. But settlers called him Crazy Snake. Harjo fought to preserve the traditional Muscogee **culture**. He was against the General **Allotment** Act. This act was designed to break up tribally owned lands and Native American traditions.

Chitto Harjo and his followers also thought the General Allotment Act broke the Treaty of 1832. This treaty had promised the Muscogee self-government. So in the winter of 1900, he and his followers set up a traditional Muscogee government in a town called Hickory Ground. US troops raided the town and broke up the Muscogee government.

Despite this, Chitto Harjo continued to speak against allotment. At a special session of the Senate in 1906, he told the history between the Muscogee and the US government. He reminded lawmakers about the treaties that promised the Muscogee the right to self-government.

Chitto Harjo in 1903

The Muscogee Today

Today, there are two Muscogee reservations. The Muscogee Nation in Oklahoma has more than 101,000 enrolled members. The Poarch Band of Creek Indians in Alabama has about 3,000 members.

The Muscogee people are working to retain their language and **culture**. Many Muscogee children learn their language in public schools. The people also gather for ceremonies.

An important celebration is the Green Corn Ceremony. During this ceremony, the people give thanks for their harvests. Women do a stomp dance, where they wear turtle shell rattles or cans around their ankles. The shells and cans make music. A sacred fire is lit. People leave the ceremony feeling spiritually fed and happy.

Today, the Muscogee live all over the world. They have many types of jobs. For example, Joy Harjo is a Muscogee poet and musician. She plays the saxophone in a band.

Joy Harjo *(left)* of the Muscogee Nation, was added to the National Women's Hall of Fame in 2022.

Glossary

adze—a tool that looks like an ax. It is used for trimming and shaping wood.

allotment—a plot of land owned by an individual. The US government's allotment policies ended the Creek's tradition of community land ownership.

awl—a pointed tool for marking or making small holes in materials, such as leather or wood.

breechcloth—a piece of hide or cloth, usually worn by men, that is wrapped between the legs and tied with a belt around the waist.

clan—a group of families in a community that has a common ancestor.

culture—the customs, arts, and tools of a nation or people at a certain time.

embroider—to decorate cloth or leather with a pattern of stitches.

geometric—made up of straight lines, circles, and other simple shapes.

gorget—a piece of armor used to protect the throat.

hide—an animal skin that is often thick and heavy.

reservation—a piece of land set aside by the government for Native Americans to live on.

sash—a wide piece of cloth used like a belt.

sinew—a band of tough fibers that joins a muscle to a bone.

tattoo—to permanently mark the skin with figures or designs.

ONLINE RESOURCES

To learn more about the Muscogee, please visit **abdobooklinks.com** or scan this QR code. These links are routinely monitored and updated to provide the most current information available.

Index